Writerly
PAPERIE

Dreamy Snowflakes
S T A T I O N E R Y   P A P E R
25 SHEETS | 5.5" x 8.5" | Half-Letter Size Paper | Simply Cut Out & Use

Simply Cut Out & Use

Simply Cut Out & Use

Simply Cut Out & Use

Simply Cut Out & Use

Simply Cut Out & Use

Simply Cut Out & Use

 Simply Cut Out & Use 

Simply Cut Out & Use

Simply Cut Out & Use

 Simply Cut Out & Use 

 Simply Cut Out & Use 

Simply Cut Out & Use

Simply Cut Out & Use

Simply Cut Out & Use

Simply Cut Out & Use

Simply Cut Out & Use

Simply Cut Out & Use